inCREDIBLE

Silly Signs

This edition published in 2006 by
Arcturus Publishing Limited
26/27 Bickels Yard, 151–153 Bermondsey Street,
London SE1 3HA

In Canada published for Indigo Books
468 King St W, Suite 500,
Toronto, Ontario M5V 1L8

ISBN-13: 978-1-84193-492-1
ISBN-10: 1-84193-492-5

Printed in China

Silly Signs covers a wide range of mistakes and mistranslations. Gathered together here are some of the best examples of what happens when not enough thought goes into a sign or a warning label.

Sometimes it is because of an amusing error in translation, or sometimes it is because the full stop is in the wrong place. More often than not, though, it is the double entendres that are guaranteed to raise a giggle.

Weird and wonderful warnings are also always good for a laugh. Whether they are stating the downright obvious, or telling you not to do something that you would never even consider, they always raise the question: Are they warning us not to do this because someone has actually done it? If so, who?

The stupid signs collected here range from the best of British to American classics, taking in examples from Egypt, Switzerland and Australia en route. It is important to remember that, ridiculous though they may seem, these are all genuine signs, notices or warnings. And it's always worth keeping your eyes peeled – there are bound to be plenty more out there.

Eat here and get gas

At restaurant-petrol stations
throughout the USA

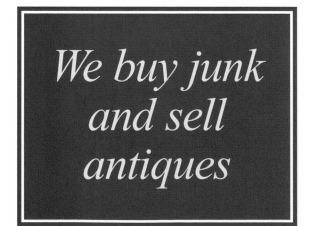

We buy junk and sell antiques

Outside a country shop

WE
CLEAN
ON THE
SPOT

Outside a South London dry cleaners

No
children
allowed

In a maternity ward, Florida

Warning:
Contains nuts

On a peanut packet

DO NOT
IRON
CLOTHES
ON BODY

On packaging for an iron

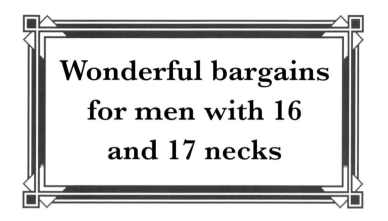

Inside a clothing store

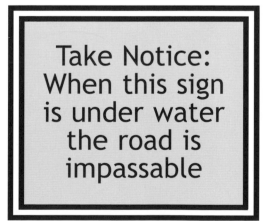

On a US highway

Elephants
please stay
in your car

A safari park notice

Toilet out of
order please
use floor
below

In a London office block

DRIVE
CAREFULLY
WE HAVE TWO
CEMETERIES
AND NO
HOSPITAL

A road sign, Branxton, USA

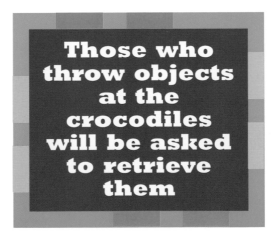

Those who
throw objects
at the
crocodiles
will be asked
to retrieve
them

A zoo sign

**Attention Dog Guardians:
Pick up after your dogs.
Thank you
Attention Dogs:
Grrrrr, bark, woof.
Good dog**

A park notice, Canada

PETS
FISH
REPTILES
SMALL ANIMALS
SENIOR CITIZENS
DISCOUNTS
HOME DELIVERY

In a pet shop's window

Swimming pool warning

A sign outside a bar

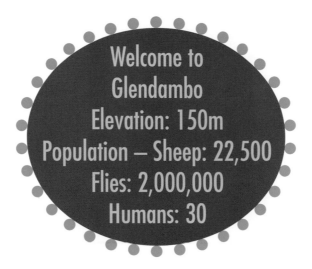

Welcome to
Glendambo
Elevation: 150m
Population – Sheep: 22,500
Flies: 2,000,000
Humans: 30

A road sign, Glendambo USA

The town hall is closed until opening. It will remain closed after being opened.

A sign outside a UK town hall

In a hotel elevator, Paris

In a mountain inn, Switzerland

Please be safe. Do not stand, sit, climb or lean on zoo fences. If you fall, animals could eat you and that might make them sick. Thank you

At a zoo, Knoxville, USA

LADIES
LEAVE
YOUR CLOTHES HERE AND
SPEND THE AFTERNOON
HAVING A
GOOD TIME

In a launderette, Rome

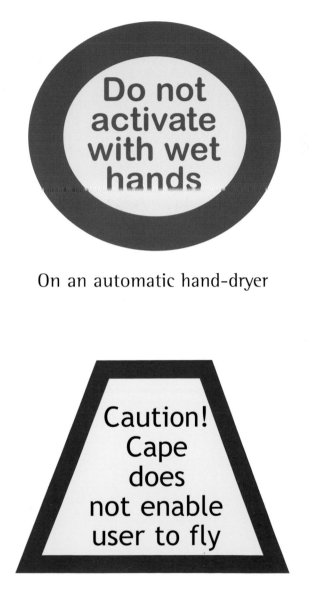

Do not activate with wet hands

On an automatic hand-dryer

Caution! Cape does not enable user to fly

Warning on a child's Batman costume

Do not drive a car or operate machinery after taking this medication

Packaging for children's cough syrup

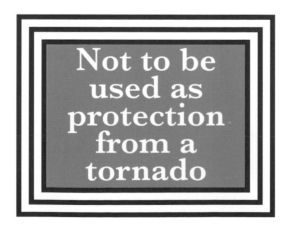

Not to be used as protection from a tornado

On a blanket from Taiwan

DO NOT USE UNDERWATER

Instructions for a toaster

**Warning:
Keep out of children**

Instructions for Korean-made kitchen knife

DO NOT USE WHILE SLEEPING

Instructions on a hairdryer

Alligator
feeding Sunday
at 3pm
Bring the kids

A zoo sign

For same day
service please give
24 hours notice

A launderette sign

After tea break
staff should
empty the teapot
and stand upside
down on the
draining board

An office kitchen, London

Automatic washing machines. Please remove all your clothes when the light goes out

A launderette sign

OPEN SEVEN DAYS A WEEK AND WEEKENDS

A sign in a restaurant

A hairdresser's sign

To aid your
enjoyment
please
eliminate dogs
and litter

A park notice

Be careful! Goats like to nibble on your clothes and butt

A petting zoo sign

Caution! Water on road during rain

A road sign, USA

Give blood –
8 billion
mosquitoes
can't be wrong

A hospital sign, USA

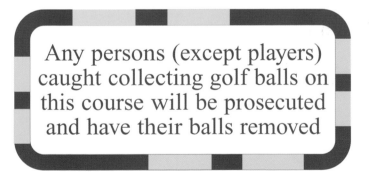

Any persons (except players)
caught collecting golf balls on
this course will be prosecuted
and have their balls removed

A sign on a golf course

A sign on a long-abandoned market site

Sign outside a farm

On a washing powder packet

Warning on a pushchair

A dry cleaner's notice

In a hotel, USA

DO NOT USE ON FOOD

Notice on dishwasher liquid packaging

If you require room service, please open door and shout, 'room service!!'

In a hotel, Egypt

Do not spray in your face

Warning on a bottle of spray paint

Kids eat free live clown every Tuesday

A restaurant sign

FOR SERIOUS INJURIES, SEEK MEDICAL ATTENTION

Instructions on a box of plasters

Instructions
Open
packet.
Eat
nuts

On a packet of peanuts

**Warning:
Can become
hot in use**

Instructions on an iron

**CAUTION
NO
WARNING
SIGNS**

A road sign

**CAUTION!
Do NOT swallow
nails! May cause
irritation!**

On a box of household nails

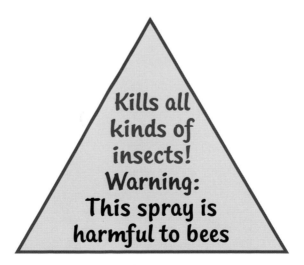

**Kills all
kinds of
insects!
Warning:
This spray is
harmful to bees**

Warning on a can of insect spray

Warning on a steering lock

Warning on a packet of juggling balls

Instructions on a toy made in China

Rules in Japanese hotel bathroom

For indoor or outdoor use only

Warning on Christmas lights

Serving suggestion: Defrost

On a frozen dinner

Warning on air conditioner

Label on bottle of baby lotion

These ear plugs are non toxic, but may interfere with breathing if caught in windpipe

Warning on ear plugs

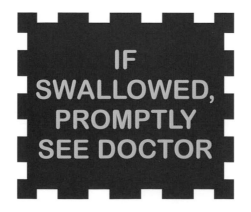

IF SWALLOWED, PROMPTLY SEE DOCTOR

Warning on 4-pack of batteries

Made in America.
Parts from Japan.
Assembled in
Mexico

On a guitar

SOME ASSEMBLY REQUIRED

Instructions on a 500-piece jigsaw puzzle

Fast food restaurant sign

Safe to use around pets and children, although it is not recommended that either be permitted to drink from toilet

Warning on toilet cleaner

Warning on an aspirin packet

Warning on sleeping tablets

Sign in a National Park, Tennessee

Road sign, USA

Warning on a coffee cup

Road sign, USA

PRIVATE
PLAYGROUND –
NO ENTRY
EXCEPT IN
EMERGENCY

Park sign, USA

Restroom
closed
Go inside

Toilet sign, USA

Road sign, Hawaii

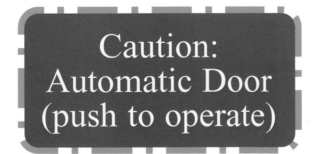

Sign on an office building

Sign in an optometrist's office

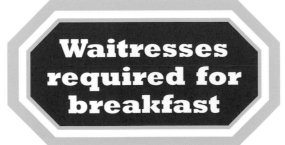

In a café window

Customers who find our waiting staff rude should see the manager

A restaurant notice

No walking, sitting or playing on the grass in this pleasure park

London park rules

Due to increasing
problems with litter
louts and vandals
we must ask anyone
with relatives buried in
the graveyard to do
their best to keep
them in order

A notice sent to residents of a UK parish

DO NOT
PUT WET CLOTHES
IN DRYERS, AS THIS
CAN CAUSE
IRREPARABLE
DAMAGE

In a laundry room

Tattoo parlour sign

A diner sign, USA

Road sign, USA

A road sign, UK

Soccer not allowed. Soccer may only be played in archery range

A park sign

Warning to young ladies – if you wear loose clothes, beware of the machinery. If you wear tight clothes, beware of the machinist

Notice in a clothes factory

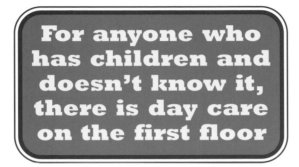

For anyone who has children and doesn't know it, there is day care on the first floor

Sign in a hotel

LADIES
MAY
HAVE A FIT
UPSTAIRS

A tailors, Hong Kong

Sign in a hotel, Greece

Dance hall sign, USA

You are
invited to take
advantage
of the
chambermaid

Sign in a hotel, Japan

It is strictly forbidden on our Black
Forest camping site that people of
different sex, for instance, men and
women, live together in one tent
unless they are married with each
other for that purpose

Sign in the Black Forest, Germany

Notice: This package contains unassembled furniture and must be assembled prior to use. Assembly instructions enclosed

Label on a furniture kit

REMOVE THIS BEFORE DRIVING

Instructions for windscreen sunshield

Warning on a bottle of dog shampoo

On a can of pepper spray

Instructions for a microwave oven

Warning on an inflatable photo frame
measuring 6x10 inches

The toilets will be partially suspended for use

Sign in a train station, Hong Kong

FITS ONE HEAD

Instructions on a shower cap

Shoes are required to eat in the canteen

Notice in a canteen

Large women's washroom, third floor

Sign in an office block, USA

The ladies of the church have cast off clothing of every kind and they may be seen in the church basement on Friday

Church jumble sale announcement

This being Easter Sunday, we will ask Mrs Lewis to come forward and lay an egg on the altar

Notice inside a church

Sign on a driveway

Road sign, India

Our
wines
leave you
nothing
to hope
for

Sign in a Swiss restaurant

Please be quiet.
We need to hear
a pin drop

Sign in a bowling alley

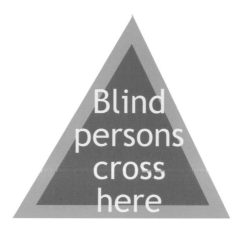

Road sign, USA

Railway crossing sign, UK

English well talking. Here speeching American

Shop sign, Majorca

Because of the impropriety of entertaining guests of the opposite sex in the bedroom, it is suggested that the lobby be used for this purpose

Sign in a hotel in Zurich

Warning on a cigarette lighter

Road sign, USA

Road sign, USA

Road sign, USA

Sign at entrance to tunnels, UK

Road sign, USA

Warning:
Unexploded
ordnance area.
Please stay within
picnic area.
Do not disturb
unidentified objects

Notice in a park

Instructions on a shampoo bottle

Instructions on a camera

Instructions for a grill

SECRET NUCLEAR BUNKER

Road sign, UK

Do not place your phone inside a microwave oven. This may damage the phone and the oven

Instructions for a mobile phone

Subway tunnel sign

Warning on hair colouring

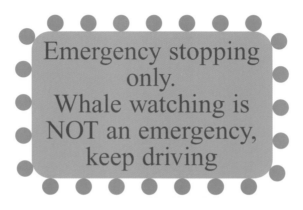

Road sign, USA

A road sign

Sign outside a dry cleaners, USA

In a shop window, Maine, USA

Sign at a loan company

Would the person who took the step ladder yesterday please bring it back or further steps will be taken

Sign in an office

Sign in a travel agents

Notice in a café window, USA

For best
results,
start with
clean bath tub
before use

On a bottle of bath tub cleaner

ANTIQUE
tables made here
daily

A sign outside a furniture shop, USA

Billboard advert for a furniture store

An advert in a dentist's practice

A road sign, Australia

Sign in a train station, China